Forbidden

MALACHI
PUBLICATIONS

FORBIDDEN 3

* BLAISE K.TSHIBWABWA *

FORBIDDEN

Blaise K. Tshibwabwa is a poet, novelist, author and public speaker whose work was discovered by Malachi Publications and admired by many.

Understanding his God Given mission on earth is his primary task!

"IF SECRECY IS LIKE HIDING;
THEN IS IT WORTH IT?
FOR
YOU CAN RUN BUT NOT HIDE…"

Blaise Tshibwabwa

BLAISE TSHIBWABWA

FORBIDDEN

MALACHI PUBLICATIONS

Toronto – Ottawa – North Charleston

PUBLISHED By Malachi Publications

Conclusion, Bibliography and Content Copyright © 2013 by Blaise Tshibwabwa

All rights reserved under International Pan-American Copyright Conventions. Published in Canada by Malachi Publications.

ISBN: 978-0-9917595-2-1

This is a work of fiction. Names, characters, businesses, places, events and incidents are either the products of the author's imagination or used in a fictitious manner. Any resemblance to actual persons, living or dead, or actual events is purely coincidental.

We ask you to respect the author's imagination and work. Illegal reproduction in part or as a whole of this work is illegal. Should you intend to reproduce this work or use parts of this work, please seek permission from the author.

Book design by BlazoBlaze

Printed and bounded in the United States of America

Twitter @BlazoBlaze

Credits to everyone at biblegateway.com who contributes regularly to the devotionals. Without you this project would not have been possible.

FORBIDDEN 8

To my wife JL (Joëlle Tshibwabwa),
I love you and thank you for your support
&
encouragement in this work and the many
more to come.

Contents

Salute   11

Forbidden   14

Finale   134

Salute

As I continue to craft this God given talent of mine, I have to say, without some of you, me staying up late, waking up early to write for the masses would not have been possible by you…

Carine & Elie Tshibwabwa, God bless you both and continue to serve the Lord diligently!

Marie-Therese & Guy Baseke, May God bless you both. I thank him for your presence in my life.

Rachel & Theo Tshibwabwa, May God bless you. May the book of Proverbs be your treasure.

Martin Tshibwabwa, Thank you for the inspiration and the continuous good laughs that I need when the keyboard and I become enemies. God Bless ya!

Jacqueline Winfield, as you strive to be there for the women with *fivefolddiva.com* my salute I give to you.

Boonmy Thongit &Warren Charlton, May the blessings of the Lord abound on you.

Joëlle & Diman Nyembwe, thank you for all the support and the kind advices!

Nadecha & Phil Hunter, thank you for listening…and that is all the time!

Maman Georgette & Papa Albert Tshakatumba, Thank you for raising a beautiful lady that I call my wife today. God Bless.

Maman Rosalie & Papa Eli Tshibwabwa (My God given Parents) I love you much and thank you for teaching me how to read and write. God Bless.

One

Hold up!
I like the feeling of the reader when they start flipping through a new work of literature. They are anxious to know if indeed this one will keep them at the edge of their seat or if it's just one of those that will take so long to finish reading and eventually abandon it on a folding table in a laundry room.

If a novel, a novella, is like the essence of having a silent conversation with unknown individuals just known by name such as Mark Twain, Charles Dickens, Alexandre Dumas and many more, then, lets have this awaited conversation.

So... a glass of wine is a bonus to have as we indulge this tale.

Karen Lancaster, a young tall brunette in her early 30's decides to shift her lifestyle and puts her Christian upbringing into the closet and swears not to step foot in a church again! Wow.

It all started with a voicemail on November 6, a girl's night out that turned to delight for some and to horror for others.

"Karen, it's Sheila, we are meeting at Ozone for 7pm then from there we shall go with the flow. Call me if you have any questions, other than that, see you there."

iMessage, Twitter, Facebook and Instagram were all part of the event. Communication was incredible. This event was going to get together five girls that had not had the chance to party together since the years of university.

"I heard Chantel got us a VIP booth at Ozone"

"How did she pull that up? I called and offered to spend minimum $500 for the night but the promoter never called back!"

"It's Chantel we talking about here!"

"Hmm, she probably dated someone who knows someone I guess"

"You ain't wrong Mirella, she dated or should I say trespassed the married life of the co-owners brother."

"You are kidding me Valerie! _and how on earth is he going to hook her up in his lounge?"

"Apparently, they had an affair too but it's so dirty that I did not even want to hear the story as soon as I heard the complexity of the matter"

"Hahaha_ you're silly girl."

"Silly ain't girl, I'm just putting into practice what my mama taught me"

"Are you kidding me? _ Hahaha, if that was the case, you would have been some preachers wife today!"

"Watch Moi arrive mon amie, soon I shall be seating front row seats at mega church conventions!"

"Oui oui, Pastor Valerie, send some deliverance Chantel's way while you're at it!"

"Wow, girl! That's wrong"

"I'm just saying; now hurry I just got a text from Karen, she's looking for a parking spot already."

"Really! I didn't know she was coming, who is coming tonight anyway?"

"You are funny, I told you it was the big five tonight, Karen, Sheila, Chantel, you and I"

"Okay there, and we got a booth on top of that; I don't know about you Mirella but I think I might call it an early night."

"Are you kidding me? _ Val! Really, why would you do that?"

"Girl, I got to get my preacher man, I am almost 35 and being single at 35 is no option!"

"Girl please, you just turned 30 last month!"

"Don't say that too loud now, the wind travels fast downtown."

"Hahaha, so you better stay late tonight and make some deliverances on all of us single ladies."

Ozone was a lounge on Delrose Street, right in the heart of downtown. A real gem with exposed brick walls, comfy lounge chairs and simple wood detailing paired with warm dim lighting that would always create a casual and friendly vibe. Once at Ozone, no need to rush out but rather stay in the welcoming zone that relaxes you into the night with a table full of martinis and much more…

The girls enjoyed the night and as per old tradition, they shut down the place and each went their way.

Two

"Val, you remind me so much of the girl in that movie with her cookie"

"Hahaha, Karen, that is so true, I keep on telling her that."

"You know what_ Karen, Mirella, I don't care who I remind you of but the fact is that my Prince has to be a preacher man and I am going to adjust myself to that!"

"All I'm saying girl is send out some deliverance our way!"

"You are so funny, so let's say he is not a preacher man but enjoys the church culture and involves himself in it, he still doesn't qualify?"

"No, come on Karen, what I mean by preacher man, is that he has to have head on his shoulders, and enjoy praying. I don't want a man who will constantly be drinking in my house and out the house and won't even know how to be a father for my kids and a husband for me."

"Oh okay, so if some brother Tyrone comes and says he wants to date and then eventually pops the question, you are alright with it?"

"Alright might be too much to say, he has to be of good character and not hide behind the church to get him a fine woman like Moi"

The girls continued mingling and laughing the day away and reminiscing on the night out they had.

"Hey Val"

"Oh, Chantel, how are you girl? Where are you?"

"I'm well. I'm at the Starbucks not far from your place."

"Really, get me a grande Latte and come on over, I got some croissants that we can eat up. Karen and Mirella are also on their way."

"Oh nice, I will text them and see what they want to drink."

The girls all gathered at Val's place and together indulged in the drinks and croissants.

"Oh Karen, I have been meaning to ask you, do you still go to that church on Osborne Avenue?"

"Yeah, I still go every now and then, who is the guy?"

"Why is it every time I refer to a spot I am asked if a guy is involved?"

"Well Chantel, considering all the marvelous things you've done back in the days of university, it is a given that there is a man in there!"

"Okay, okay, I am going to tell, but please don't tell."

"Okay, Ladies, I think we should go indoor, the backyard might not be the best place to have a top secret conference."

The girl laughed and off they went to the basement to listen to the revelation Chantel had to unveil.

"Before I say anything, girls don't hate me, it happened and I am done with it, I am turning the page and will not step in those grounds again, I feel horrible."

"Chantel, don't worry, haven't we heard it all with you and seen it all!"

"I had an affair with this guy and he told me that he goes to church, the church on Osborne Ave."

"What's his name?"

"Ryan Makowski"

"What? _ Chantel, please tell me you are joking?"

"No, that's his name, Ryan Makowski and he owns an auto body and maintenance shop too."

"Did he tell you what he does at church?"

"No, all he said is that he goes to that church and I told him that church ain't really my cup of tea, all he replied was I don't blame you."

"Chantel, I don't know how to tell you this but he is the young adults pastor of the church, and just last week, he gave me an invitation for this event they are hosting and asked me to come because it is to help single women and single men not to involve themselves prior to marriage."

"Well, brother Makowski is surely practicing something but it ain't what he preaches fo sho."

"Val_!"

"What? I 'm just saying"

"True, true, I think we should all go to that event and hear what he's going to talk about, because seriously I don't even know why I go to church! If a man who claims to serve God can't even refrain himself from fooling around."

"He is a man and I think he was just practicing the Song's of Solomon Hahaha"

"Mirella, you are crazy girl!"

"So, Karen, are you off to your meeting later on tonight?"

"It's not funny and he is the one talking tonight, grrrr, I don't know, this is just_I don't know_."

"Val, are you still going to be a preacher man's wifey, now that you heard this?"

"Damn right girl friend! I'm done this weird life of ups and downs; if today I was to meet that Makowski man, if he told me the truth about what happened, before he met me, I will give him his chance, as long as he gives it up."

"Hmm, I don't think so, all I know is that I am not going to church any more, that's it for me. I can't take this."

"Karen, come on, it's just a man; one man; not all men. And beside, it's not like his married or anything."

"That is true girls, but the problem is that he is engaged to the song leader!"

"Oh_Oh_Oh! Girl, No, No, you did not just say that! No! That is unacceptable!"

"That is pathetic! Karen, I did not know, I am so sorry, I did not know."

"Chantel, if he did not say, how would you know?"

"The point is girls, stop giving your cookie to just any man you meet out there!"

"Here we go again, and since when did you become Santa Val_ hahaha"

Three

Let's put the wine down. I think for this part, a cup of tea might be more helpful. It looks a bit cliché, girls who hang out together since university, went to all sorts of parties and did as they were led by their hearts. Time went by, some outgrew the playing around and some decided to continue!

It's something when a man tells a woman not to fool around with men. Women have always wanted to understand men. Well…

"I want to thank each of you for accepting the invitation on coming out to support our group. As we all know, life as a human is not easy, and as a Christian it is even harder to conquer the various trials and temptations that come our way and those that we also go dig for because we did not listen to what God told us in the first place.

I would like to invite our speaker for the evening, Reverend Jeff Al Bareck"

The crowd responded by applaud as this one made his way to the microphone. Surprisingly, he was not dressed like the usual reverend would; he had khaki pants on, a white shirt with timberland boots. He had his ipad with him and waved to the crowd as he made his way to the front.

"Thank you Ryan, and thank you all for being here tonight. Thank you for taking the time to come and gather here and listen to me voice out a few things. I can see that we have a lot of lovely ladies in the building and lots of handsome young men too! _Now please, don't take notes, this is a very informal sharing that I am going to do, and I am not your typical reverend. I guess you can see already by the way I dress.

Don't worry about taking notes, at the end, my assistants Raphael, Patricia and Sherry will give out booklets with the main points.

What I am about to share with you, I called it Forbidden!

Ladies, I ask you to bare with me because I'm going to pick on you for a bit and then we shall switch it over to the men!"

The ladies in the hall clapped and cheered on "Amen to that!"

"First things first, I cannot stop and will not stop stressing this – Men, Take good care of your wife's! She is a gift from God, if you think I am joking or making it up_read Proverb 18 vs. 22.

Women, you are called woman because you are bone of his bones, flesh of his flesh, you were taken out of man_ see it in Genesis 2 vs 23. So, take good care of your husband's too!

If you are not married yet, it still applies to you. Take good care of yourself; don't bed hop or mouth hop! Oh! Don't give me round eyes now, this is real talk.

Now, where am I getting with this? Like seriously Rev. we know that, you must be telling me _ and I appreciate the fact that you know that but then tell me, why do we have too many sisters saying -that guy does not deserve me; I don't deserve his sorry ass! Yep, I said it, let's be real here, that's why we have these meetings, it's to be real with each other and to tackle what needs to be tackled!

I don't' know, if you have ever taken the time to ask yourself these questions:

1-   Why do women cheat?
2-   Why do men cheat?
3-   Why is talking about sex taboo? Why is it almost if not always considered Forbidden in most households?
4-   Will you make a difference? Are you making a difference?

Aha! I see people smiling, good; it means we are making progress here!

And by the way, if you have cheated on your husband, on your wife, on your fiancé (e)…my friend, you better ask the Lord for forgiveness and go see your partner and ask for forgiveness, go see the person with whom you were involved in this wrongful sinful act and excuse yourself for not telling them you had commitments elsewhere.

Once a cheat, always a cheat I can feel people telling me, wow, I like this crowd_ Hahaha,

Well, let's answer the questions and see if we can get to the bottom of this, and by the way, don't hesitate to continue enjoying your drinks, this is very informal, I am not preaching, we are having a conversation, hence the reason why I am only holding a mic. and walking around to make sure no one is sleeping on me_ Hahaha I'm just joking.

I will start by the issue of sex being taboo. For your own information, in case you have not had the time to flip through your bible, the bible does talk about sex in all forms. By that I mean, it will tell you the pros and cons.

So, talking about it is not taboo, we have future parents in here, some of you already have kids from previous relationships, some of you while you were growing up, no one took the time to seat with you and talk about this, you had to learn from friends, the radio, the television, books and all sorts of other sources that might not have been the best place to get the information from.

Let's get this right, we are not here to blame, finger point or single out anyone! We are just here to keep it real and push some sense into each other.

I hope you all agree when I say that talking about sex is not taboo. Talking about sex is a reality that we all need to be confortable to address with our kids, siblings, parents, friends and pastors should the need arise.

As an individual, there is only one way of practicing safe sex, and that is by not having pre marital sex, by not having a same sex relationship and when married by not cheating on their spouse.

You laugh, and you argue with me saying, are you out of your mind rev? If I don't have sex before marriage, how am I going to handle it in my marriage?

Well, ask yourself this question_ where you taught how to laugh? Where you taught how to fall in love with another? Aha, you are laughing now, because it came naturally. Right, it is human nature. So don't lie to yourself about trying to practice none-sense before marriage that might lead you into adultery once married."

"Al Bareck all the way!" some lady shouted from across the floor and giving a high five to her friend.

"I mean, I ain't coming up with my own stuff here, it's black on white, check it out in 1 Corinthians 7:1-3 –Each man should have his own wife, and each woman should have her own husband because of sexual immorality. The husband should meet his wife's sexual needs, and the wife should do the same for her husband.

Clear and simple. It did not say: men meet your girlfriend's sexual needs, and women meet your boyfriend's sexual needs. It did not say men: meet your wife's and the friend of your wife's sexual needs!

So why on earth are you men and women sleeping with each other like you are changing movies on Netflix or something? _ Come on now! Don't give me the silence treatment because I am talking about what you thought would never be spoken of in a Christian gathering! Today, we have pastors, deacons, sisters and brothers alike hoping in beds all over the city!

We have parents, scared to seat their kids down and tell them the truth about sexual immorality!

Shame on you!

And we have too many children, who have had the opportunity of having their parents seat them down and tell them the truth about sexual immorality but yet still go out there and do it!

Shame on you!

What you think is Forbidden is not Forbidden! Not talking about these issues is the reason we have women not wanting to get married anymore. Because you men are labelled as players! All you do is sweet talk women, try and sleep with them and then flee away like a dog running out of a grave yard, and then you are shocked women refer to you as dogs! Total mess!

Fellas, come on now, don't you feel that you owe yourself more respect?

You even have the audacity of hiding behind the church to scoop women! God forbid that next time you commit an act of sexual immorality the thunder of heaven doesn't consume you!

Some of you, your parents, siblings, friends gave you the best advise one can get, yet you go around sleeping with women, you go ahead sleeping with men, and when society labels you, off you are running to the pastors office asking for prayer. Are you still with me?"

"Yes we are" the crowd responded with applaud.

"Thank you, Hahaha, let's continue, why do women cheat? Why, why, why?

I mean it is said that a women is worth more than gold, diamonds and any precious stone that humans will ever discover on earth! So why are you allowing yourself to depreciate like that?

Do not let that jezebel spirit take control of you! Cast it out in the name of Jesus. For those of you who don't know Jezebel, I strongly suggest that you take the time to inform yourself on it. I won't go there today, since we are on a limited time frame."

"No, no" the women in the audience chanted. Then Valerie stood and voiced "Rev. I think that my fellow women are open to hear what you have to say on Jezebel unless it also features in the booklets?"

"Actually it doesn't, so by demand, I will give you a summarized run down of Jezebel."

"Thank you Rev." The women chanted together with applaud.

" I like that, you see how women are open and willing to hear the word of the Lord! I hope men will be also responsive when their turn comes_ Hahaha, I'm just playing; okay, so who is Jezebel?"

FORBIDDEN

Four

"Jezebel means, "chaste, free from carnal connection"; but by nature she was a most licentious woman. She was a voluptuary, with all the tawdry arts of a wanton woman. No name could have been more inappropriate for such a despised female.

Jezebel was no ordinary woman. Such was her demeanor that she attracted immediate attention. Though by no means an attractive personage, she was invested by her extraordinary force of character and her appalling fate with a tragic grandeur, which belongs to no other woman of the Bible.

While the Bible does not analyze or even portray her character, but simply sets forth the events in which she bore so prominent a part, yet as we read between the lines we cannot fail to see her as a woman of prodigious force of intellect and will.

The sacred narrative does not record that she possessed any of the finer, nobler feminine qualities. She knew nothing of the restraint of higher principles. Savage and relentless, this proud and strong-minded woman carried out her foul schemes.

A gifted woman, she prostituted all her gifts for the furtherance of evil, and her misdirected talents became a curse.

Persuasive, her influence was wrongly directed. Resolute above other women, she used her strength of character to destroy a king and her own offspring, as well as pollute the life of a nation.

Jezebel was an ardent idolater!

Jezebel was a dominating wife! (She is the heathen woman who married Ahab, king of Northern Israel, and who in so doing was guilty of a rash and impious act, which resulted in evil consequences.) Jezebel became the feared commander in Israel and not the cowardly husband she could wrap around her thumb.

It may be that Ahab was more luxury-loving and sensual than cruel, but under the complete domination of a ruthless woman he was forced to act against his finer feelings. His culpability in this hideous drama lies chiefly in his using his personal power as a means to Jezebel's wicked ends.

For without Ahab's authority, Jezebel would have been a serpent without fangs. In this marriage, Ahab was the weaker vessel with a wife who mocked at his conscientious scruples and bound him in all wickedness as with strong chains.

In Matthew 7 vs. 16 to 20, it says a corrupt tree cannot bring forth good fruit. This jezebel is referred to as a corrupt tree too! Jezebel was rotten root and branch, and thus everything connected with her was contaminated.

How appropriate are the lines of Shakespeare as we think of Jezebel who, in her strength of character, lust for power, remorseless rejection of godliness, and unshrinking and resolute activity to abolish all that interferes with the fulfillment of her wicked designs.

A strong adversary, an inhuman wretch, incapable of pity, void and empty from every drachm of pity. Her offspring imbibed and continued the wickedness they grew up in. Jezebel's evil influence was revived in her daughter Athaliah of Judea. Her malign character reappears in her eldest son, Ahaziah, who, like his idolatrous mother, was a devout worshiper of Baal.

Her second son, Jehoram or Joram, was another image of his mother—further corrupt fruit from a corrupt tree. It was Jehoram, who heard from the lips of Jehu who had been raised up to obliterate the Ahab dynasty, that there would be no peace in Israel, 2 kings 9 vs. 22 says - so long as the whoredoms of thy mother Jezebel and her witchcrafts are so many.

The death of Jezebel had "stirred up to work wickedness in the sight of the Lord" revealed her to be as incapable of remorse as of fear.

There was no sign of repentance in her. Jezebel's son and grandson met Jehu in the bloodstained vineyard Naboth had once possessed. Jehu slew Jezebel's son, the king of Israel, and her grandson was overtaken in flight and was slain.

The still proud, defiant woman knew her last hour was not far away; she took time to arrange her hair and paint her face, and looked out at a window to greet Jehu as he passed by. Perhaps Jezebel did not paint her face from any motive of coquetry or vanity. She knew that death was ready to take her.

Therefore, she determined to die like a queen.... As Cleopatra, when about to die, robed herself in festal garments, so Jezebel painted her eyes with antimony and placed her jeweled crown upon her head; then, mounting to the palace tower, she watched the thundering advance of Jehu's chariot.
This one touch of grandeur in her foul life gave rise to the bitter taunt, "a painted Jezebel," which came into vogue in England during the sixteenth century when, as Edith Deen reminds

us, "painting the face was accepted as *prima-facie* evidence that a woman had loose morals. Certainly no woman's name in history has become so commonly accepted as a synonym for wickedness.

Ere we turn from our portrait of one of the most wicked women who ever breathed, there are one or two lessons to glean from her deeply stained record. No matter from what angle we approach the life of Jezebel she stands out as a beacon to both nations and individuals that the wages of sin is death. Further, from this great tragic figure of literature and of history we learn how important it is for the influence of a wife and mother to be on the side of all that is good and noble.

As Ahab's evil genius, Jezebel was the absolute negation of all God meant woman to be, namely, a true helpmeet of man. Ahab, we read, was "stirred up" by Jezebel but stirred up in the wrong direction. When a man marries a woman because of her beauty or forceful personality, or marries a wicked woman or one opposed to his religion, he usually courts sorrow, heartache and disappointment. Jezebel retained her obstinate, unbending character to the very end. The death of the man whose life she polluted brought no repentance. What a difference story would have been written if only she had learned how to stir up her husband and children to love God and follow good works.

Her misdirected talents, however, brought upon her a curse. The evil she perpetrated was done under the guise of religion, just as the cruelties of the Inquisition and the tortures of Smithfield were.

Evil and craft and godlessness bring their own reward, and the wicked reap what they sow. Retribution overtook Jezebel when her body was thrown out of the window to be torn and mangled, and then eaten by dogs. As a daughter of the devil, she suffers a worse retribution in the realms of the doomed. There are those who reject such a lurid description of the fate of the wicked who, like Jezebel, defy and deny God, but the divine Word still stands, that Christ is to be revealed from heaven to take vengeance on those who spurn God and who reject the saving Gospel of His beloved Son.

This is my run down on Jezebel! So women, adjust your lifestyle. You are worth a lot!"

Five

"Men! Oh men, men, men, don't be the Jack Sparrow of your relationship!

Many people think that the Bible has very little to say about abuse, and yet there are countless bible verses which speak clearly and definitely on the subjects of domestic abuse and domestic violence.

Quite often, if we as victims approach and confide in an elder, priest, or member of our Church, hoping for some support and encouragement, we can leave feeling even guiltier and trapped than we did formerly. We may be told that the abuse is due to our own lack of submissiveness, or our own sinfulness, that we would not suffer if our faith was greater, or that we will be rewarded in the next life for the suffering we experience in this one (Like What? Are you kidding me?).

I have heard of women who have been told earnestly by their pastor that it would be better for them to die at the hands of their abusive husband than to seek a separation and protection for their children!

When talking to Church members we have to realize that the understanding of Domestic Abuse is still in its infant stages in many Churches, and that the majority of people (including elders and pastors) still hold basic misconceptions regarding the dynamics of an abusive relationship and have formed their opinions less on what Scripture says, and more on those myths generally held in society.

An added hurdle is to be found especially in the more fundamental denominations, where the mistaken belief is often that such things may happen "in the World", but not in a good Christian home! Sorry to burst your bubble, there is abuse in Christian homes, and that has to STOP!

Ladies and gents, I know these topics are at times considered taboo in some denominations! But in order for us to move well, we got to tackle what is on the way.

Any church leader that counsels an abused woman "Cook better," "Don't push your husband's buttons," "Pray harder," or worst yet, "It is God's will," obviously doesn't know the heart of God. In fact, I would suggest that the ministers pray harder themselves for the correct interpretation of the Word of God.

Their misunderstanding of how to "rightly divide the Word" is causing many Christian women to abandon their relationship with our Creator. In doing so, all hope of eternal salvation is lost.

I mean, I hope and really hope that all of you agree that God is not a male sexist, who gives earthly men the green light to dominate, control, abuse, violate and destroy the souls of their mates. No, this is the erroneous teaching of men who learned from society and various mediums how *not* to be a real man. Only the Word of God can teach men how to be the men that God intended them to be.

Look unto Jesus Christ, did He abuse, dominate, control, demean, violate, strike or place women in compromising positions?

What scripture – points to Jesus verbally abusing women and children? Where in scripture does God permit a man to rape his wife, and reward him for doing so?

No minister can honestly say abusing your wife is permissible. If so, I wish someone would point them out to me – they won't. And why? Because scriptures that condone violence against one another don't exist.

In fact, you will read just the opposite, "Love one another" (John 13:35). This is not a plea, but a COMMAND. I challenge anyone that reads the bible to show me where the scripture says, "If your wife burns dinner again tonight, slap her silly."

Better yet, show me where the Word says, "Lock her in the closet all day if she doesn't obey you." Still yet, "Strip her of her self-esteem, take away her money, and all of her support." Where in scripture does it say, "Teach your sons how to abuse women or abuse men?" Does the bible teach that? Or, "Shoot her in the head if she keeps on mouthing off."

Nor will you find scriptures that give a woman the right to verbally abuse her husband, and physically harm her children. If your husband isn't measuring up to your human standards, God does not suggest, "Scratch his eyes out, and hit him with a frying pan." Nor does he say, "Verbally blast him and make him feel as small as you can."

Jesus our Lord left an example of how we should conduct ourselves as children of God. The foundations of His teachings are based on love, "For God so loved the world that He gave His only begotten Son…" (John 3:16) God is LOVE! And His commandments are not grievous, but intended for our good. *The Word becomes an inconvenience when the flesh desires to have its own way.* What happens then is – the Word is twisted to suit the fancies and whims of mortal man, who from the beginning desired to be a god – to take the place of Almighty God.

Instead of arguing about what scriptures do say, maybe it is time to point out what they don't say. When dominating and controlling husbands use scripture to abuse their wives, they are filling in the blanks, where there are no blanks. What they are doing is akin to adding and subtracting to and from the Word of God. And that process brings about a curse.

Just look at our homes today, wouldn't you say they are cursed in many ways? They are cursed not by God, but by their actions and misquoting of Holy Scriptures. *This is cause and effect, reaping what is being sown."*

Six

"And this brings us to the end of my sharing for tonight." Rev. Al Bareck said as he gave the microphone back to Ryan with the audience applauding.

"Thank you all, thank you Rev. thank you. This sharing went straight to the spot. And I pray we all act on what we heard, you are free to stick around, we have the place booked up to 11pm"

The girls looked at each other, laughed a bit and then began to walk towards the exit.

"Well Valerie, I guess that gives you a good broad picture of what you want to get into."

"Surprisingly it does, I should attend another of his sessions, the poster said that he has open mic. nights, where he answers questions from the audience."

"Chantel, what's your call on this?"

"Well, I feel really bad now after what happened between me and Ryan and mostly that he is engaged! I just hope that he will come forth and excuse himself and that he does the same with his fiancée!"

"He better, if he don't, I will take care of it!"

"Karen! You are not taking care of anything"

"Mirella, it's just wrong! No wonder we call them dogs!"

"Hahaha, girl, Al Bareck got me laughing when he said that men flee like dogs out of a grave yard!"

"Hahaha, he nailed it on extra target"

"Girls, I honestly don't know how I will step in church and look at the innocent girl sing in front and meanwhile her man cheated on her, who knows if you are not the first one?"

"Karen, come on take it easy, let us pray about it"

"I think we should call up Rev. Al Bareck and ask him what he thinks about that!"

"Mirella, really? You are going to pick up your phone and say what?"

"I will say, this is Valerie Sinkala and we have a real scenario here of a friend sleeping with an engaged man. And he so happens to be very involved in church"

"Hahaha, he will say, cast that Jezebel spirit Ouuuuuuuut!"

"Hahaha" the girls burst in laughter and continued walking towards the subway station.

Seven

"If you just joined us, you did the right choice! This is your host DJ Mutoba and welcome to the BlazoBlaze show on Church-Vibe 84.4 FM; before we open the phone lines, we have with us Reverend Jeff Al Bareck in the studio and he will be answering questions from you our listeners. Rev. Al Bareck_"

"Can I call you Rev?" DJ Mutoba asked

"No problem, call me Rev.; call me Jeff Al B.; it's all good, we just give God the glory in all we do _seen"

"Nice, I like that, Rev Jeff Al B. but just so the listeners don't get lost here, Rev. Al Bareck is from our beautiful city, born and raised, born again and raised again in this very city"

"That's right! Toronto has always been home to me."

"Well, well, the lines are about to open, we're just going to take a break and after that we going talk with Rev. Al Bareck on the BlazoBlaze show_"

A few minutes passed giving time for the Rev. to freshen up and have his material on hand before the phone lines would open.

"Welcome back to the BalzoBlaze show, this is your host DJ Mutoba, and we have Rev. Jeff Al B_ most commonly known as Rev. Al Bareck; _So Rev. thank you for accepting our invitation and congratulations on your Juno Award that you received with the Zion Gospel Choir."

"Thank you, it's an honor."

"Alright, I can see the lines flashing _ Church-Vibe 84.4 you are on the line, please introduce yourself"

"Hey DJ Mutoba, this is Kristi calling from Milton"

"Milton wins the first call today, I'm good girl_don't be shy shoot your question away to the Rev."

"Thank you, morning Rev"

"Hey Kristi, I'm listening go right ahead"

"Cool, my favorite movie is Pretty Woman, without a doubt! I watched it twice in one night when my friends and I sneaked back into the theater when we were in college. This is the ultimate chick flick. Julia Roberts had it made—a sexy, rich man wanted to take care of her and lavish attention on her with no strings attached.

Of course, in 1990, the only way Hollywood could get away with portraying that ideal was to make the main character a prostitute—a likable one you'd want to be friends with—but a prostitute nonetheless.

As if the picture of a woman who was in control of her sexuality and using it for her benefit was somehow unbecoming for the average woman.

Now we've grown into a more sophisticated sexual freedom. My girlfriends and I meet eligible single men at trendy clubs downtown. Most of the men there are stockbrokers or successful lawyers and doctors. We're adults with disposable incomes and time on our hands.

I was nervous the first time I had a guy I met at a club over to my condo. I poured some drinks, we talked about our families and work and then we messed around until he had to go home for work the next day.

I recall looking in the mirror the next morning and strangely not recognizing my own face right away, but I also remember the rush of feeling empowered. Every time I hook up with a guy, I feel as if I break through some other barrier. It's as if I'm in control of my life in a way I couldn't have imagined before.

I'm not actually sleeping with these guys. Some of my girlfriends do, but I'm just out to have fun. It wasn't that long ago when only men were allowed to have fun like this, but this is an equal opportunity planet. More power to us! So my question is what is your feel on that, any advice, suggestion?"

"Well Kristi, it's a good thing I was taking notes Hahaha, just joking, on a serious note, it is true, the sexual revolution drastically changed how women viewed their sexuality. In the past, women hid their sexuality under restrictive clothing and severe social codes.

Now we flaunt it. Women used to be envious of men's supposed sexual freedom and the apparent power it gave them. Now we have that same "freedom," but where has it gotten us?

1-Legalized abortion—A world in which even if a woman wants to keep her baby, her partner has no responsibility to stand beside her and support her. Too many women feel alone and pressured to abort their children. So ask yourself, is that freedom?

2-Disappointment—Relationships in which men won't commit because they don't have to. Why buy the cow when you can get the milk for free?

3-Emotional baggage—Past physical attachments, emotional scars and the weight of guilt so that women can't enter fully into their marriages or the relationships God intended for them.

4-Disrespect—In a world of sexual freedom, women are often treated like (surprise, surprise) sex objects. When was the last time a man held the door for you? And, I am sure we can count it on just one hand!

5-Expectations—Just because a man buys you dinner doesn't mean you owe him sex—not after one date, four dates, six months or two years.

We're no better off sexually than our mothers, fathers and grandparents. We may feel a sense of control, but it comes at a very high price—the price of our clean consciences, of our whole relationships, of our sexual purity.

God wants women to experience the powerful, intoxicating pleasures of their sexuality. Yet he has specific parameters in which that experience should take place—in a monogamous, marital relationship, one man and one woman, for life. Satan exploits a woman's sexuality by enticing her to express herself sexually outside of God's ideal—through promiscuity, premarital sex or adultery."

"Wow, thank you Rev. that is powerful, so I guess it's Sexual freedom God's way, no other way Kristi"

"Kristi are you still on the line girl?"

"Yes, I am, I'm taking notes too_"

"Nice, but Rev. would you mind backing that up with some scriptures that we can refer ourselves to?"

"Certainly, we think we feel empowered. God says we are enslaved—either to sin or to righteousness see Romans 6:16

We tell ourselves we're in control when we use sex in relationships (since we have what men want). God calls that kind of control self-deception see 1 Corinthians 3:18–19.

The world assures us sexual freedom is life's highest reward. God warns us that we will reap what we sow. See Galatians 6:7.

Just imagine, CDC estimates that there are approximately 19 million new [sexually transmitted disease] infections occurring each year.

You, my brothers and sisters, were called to be free. But do not use your freedom to indulge the flesh see Galatians 5:13"

"Interesting, and for the record CDC is the Centre for Disease Control_ Time for a quick break and before we do that, Kristi, where did you just get your blaze?"

"I got it on the BlazoBlaze show with DJ Mutoba at Church-Vibe 84.4 FM"

"Yeuuup, yeuuuup"

"Allo, Val, it's Mirella are you listening to the BalzoBlaze show?"

"I am girl; I'm on hold with my house phone_"

"Welcome back to the BlazoBlaze show, this is your host DJ Mutoba and we are answering your questions with Reverend Al Bareck right here, live on Church-Vibe 84.4FM_next caller on the line you are live, introduce yourself and shoot away"

"Yes! Thank you, it's Miranda from Etobicoke and I wonder if my situation is a cause for a divorce because I just don't know anymore. I am still so indescribably shocked that I'm not even sure if it really happened. Of course, I know it did. It's impossible to dream up something like this.

My husband and I are leaders in the student ministry—He's a coach for our daughter's softball team and a deacon at our church. I wonder for how long he had this going on? Is he an addict like the perverts who fill the strip joints? I mean he is my husband!

Before yester night, I had no reason to suspect my husband of doing anything as vulgar and repulsive as paying for smut. He is my best friend. We have a wonderful marriage. We talk to each other about everything. We spend time together.

Our sex life isn't like it was when we were younger, but I thought it was healthy and normal. In fact, he just surprised me with a trip to Hawaii for our tenth wedding anniversary. I get nauseous whenever I think of him fantasizing about all these women whenever we made love.

Then, I get angry. All this time, and I had no idea.

What kind of a husband surprises his wife with a wedding anniversary trip to Hawaii and then downloads porn off the Internet in our own home?

And what am I going to tell my parents?

Your son-in-law is a pervert?

He's not the person we thought he was all these years?

It will absolutely break their hearts. I can't handle this, God. We had a good … we have a good marriage. I still want to believe we have a good marriage. That's why there must be some sort of mistake. It just can't be as bad as it seems. Please, God, what did I do wrong?"

"Miranda, thank you for your call and I am glad that you got through the phone lines. To answer to your situation, the allure of pornography makes no distinction between Christian and non-Christian men.

Unfortunately, as wives, mothers and sisters, women want to believe pornography could never be a problem for the men in their lives. However, we can't afford to be naive when it comes to understanding the nature of sin and its addictive qualities.

First, we have to admit that pornography addiction can happen in Christian homes, and it does. Frequently.

Second, we must see that pornography is a true addiction—those who are involved in it may say they want to stop, even try desperately to stop, but they are often powerless to escape it without help. This is not to exonerate them from responsibility. Pornography is a deliberate choice that brings shame and pain to families.

Third, women should recognize that their husbands need help, sometimes-clinical aid, to break free from their addiction to pornography.

Fourth, women cannot take the burden of accountability onto themselves. Men need other Christian men to hold them brutally accountable for their choices. Resources like Promise Keepers specialize in Internet accountability. You can also search online for Internet filters or accountability software.

At the same time, women whose husbands look at pornography need to find someone to talk to about the grief associated with this violation against their marriage.

The worst scenario is for a woman to feel so shamed and rejected by the discovery of her husband's addiction that she refuses to ask for help from the church or other family-centered crisis counseling. Pornography, like all sin, thrives in darkness. Bring it into the light by seeking help.

Create a climate of honesty in your home so that even if your husband fails, you can pray together for victory over this sin. It may feel very painful for you to talk and pray about this topic since you are the one who feels wronged, yet love is an endless act of dying to oneself.

Begin to pray for your sons or the young men in your life. Our culture is so sexually saturated, brimming with visual temptation for men, that men must fight proactively to guard their minds.

Understand that the enemy wants to hook our sons early and hard. They need to hear from Christian men how they should start now to set up boundaries in their lives."

"Are you following me Miranda?"

"Yes I am Rev. I am but it's hard, I just feel like giving it all up!"

"Miranda, never give up. The Holy Spirit can bring freedom see John 8:32; with God there is always hope for healing for your husband and your marriage.

He will bring to light what is hidden in darkness and will expose the motives of the heart. See 1 Corinthians 4:5. God Bless you dear."

"Thank you Rev. Thank you."

"Alright, one more call before we go on commercial break, Rev. don't hesitate to drink some of that water!"

"Hahaha_ DJ Mutoba, thank you, I surely need some"

"Church-Vibe 84.4, caller you are on the line"

"Morning DJ Mutoba, Morning Rev. My name is Tammy and I am calling from Vaughn and I have a bit of a situation, I recently met a friend and I was talking about it to my friend at work, I will just refer to him as John Doe and I did not know what to say when he asked me the question if the new guy I was seeing goes to church. I mean, I've finally found someone I really like, and things are going great.

Still, John Doe is my partner at work, and he and his wife know everything there is to know about me. They know I grew up in church. And they also know I dated a few guys from the church singles group. But there just wasn't any chemistry.

I had always dreamed that God would have the perfect person picked out for me and deliver him right to my door.

However, I was fast approaching the big 3–0, and it still hadn't happened. In fact, I had almost given up, figuring I was destined to be single for the rest of my life, and then this guy came along. We met at the gym.

I would have married him on the spot for his calves alone. However, it was his smile that really got to me.

We kept running into each other in the mornings before work, and he finally asked me to go out one weekend. We talked for hours that first night, as if we'd known each other forever. He was wonderful.

Over the next few weeks, as my relationship with him grew, John Doe started to ask me more questions. "Does he know you're a Christian? Have you told him about your faith?" I fended him off with a few cursory answers. "He didn't grow up in church like you and I did," I told him. "But I think he gets it, or at least he's pretty close." John Doe didn't seem satisfied with my answer.

Truthfully, something inside of me cringed when I said it. But I'm not going to let anything or anyone spoil my happiness. Who's to say he isn't the man I dreamed of all along? He'll probably become a Christian at some point in our relationship, and then everything will be perfect."

"Wow, love, love, love, do you believe love stories like Isaac and Rebekah's can happen?"

"Yes Rev, I do"

"Okay, two people who aren't even from the same country brought together by God's hand. But oh, the things we're willing to believe in the midst of a man-drought. When the phone isn't ringing because no one's calling. When we spend another Valentine's Day with the cat.

There's a "certain age," you know, past which all of our mothers' friends believe the odds for us finding the man of our dreams plummet.

Add to the mix the complication of a Christian woman looking for a Christian man—and the situation becomes even more discouraging. We begin to convince ourselves that we somehow missed God's best. Maybe that's the problem.

We just weren't open before—our standards were too high. And so, now we're not being desperate; we're being open. Unfortunately, that's when we begin to rationalize whatever we want to fit the ideal.

He's not super-spiritual, but show me a man who is!

He has such great potential—he needs someone like me to encourage him.

It's important to note that we won't change God's mind, even though we can list all sorts of factors in favor of our decision to marry outside of our convictions. The Bible's warning not to marry a non-Christian is very clear see 2 Corinthians 6:14. Think about it. How will you celebrate Christmas and Easter?

Or discipline your children?

Will your husband understand wanting to tithe from your joint account?

Will he mind if you're gone for part of every Sunday?

How do you feel about having a quiet time alone?

The issues range from minor to major. If you're single and lonely, God knows it. If you're approaching a certain age, God knows how old you are. And he is not worried. The important thing is not to be married … it's to be married to the right person. And God can bring that person unexpectedly, just as he did for Isaac and Rebekah.

Feelings and emotions can be disastrously misleading in this area. That's why we have to hold onto God's Word, not a wish list, and let God dictate our decision whether or not to marry someone.

He is Mr. Almost for now, but perhaps with one change he could become Mr. Right. Before your heart rides off into the sunset … hold out for someone who has the same goal and the same faith. By not settling, you will have peace of mind in knowing you did what was right for yourself, your children and, yes, even Mr. Almost.

Remember this Tammy; do not be yoked together with unbelievers. For what do righteousness and wickedness have in common? Or what fellowship can light have with darkness? _2 Corinthians 6:14"

"Thank you Rev. but it's easier said than done"

"It is Tammy and that is why the Holy Spirit is there to help you"

"Amen! We wish you all the best Tammy and we're going to take a break, keep it locked right here on Church-Vibe 84.4FM"

Eight

"Welcome back to the BalzoBlaze show on Church-Vibe 84.4FM, I'm your host DJ Mutoba and with us in studio answering your questions is the one and only Reverend Jeff Al Bareck_ Hello, you are live on the air who is this?"

"It's Robert from Toronto_"

"Oh, the men are waking up, nice nice, God bless you brother"

"Thank you DJ Mutoba, patience pays Hahaha"

"You are right, go right ahead ma man, Rev. Al B. is ready"

"Thanks, Morning Rev, I have a question that I think a lot of men may have, and that is the one of marriage, can you give me_ us a rundown of the way God intended it to be, because it's hard these days to find the right woman!"

"I hear wedding bells! Well Robert, before I explain further take note of these scriptures and read them in your spare time Song of Songs 8:6–7, Genesis 2:18–25; Matthew 19:1–9; and Hebrews 13:4.

The passage in Song of Songs, perhaps as powerfully as any other in the entire Bible, defines and describes for modern readers God's intentions when he invented and defined the institution of marriage.

Marriage as a concept lies deep within our collective psyche. Preschoolers role-play the family unit as part of their playground fun. Preteen girls dream of the day when they'll walk down the aisle in a flowing white gown. Matchmaking businesses and Web sites thrive as people look for that elusive one perfect person to know and love for the rest of their lives.

The vast majorities of adults who live in Western cultures either are or have been or someday intend to be married.

Such hopefulness in the face of a consistent 50 percent divorce rate! And yet, despite the well-publicized antics of the Hollywood set, marriage remains one of the key building blocks of family life and society as a whole. And that's just what God intended.

The language in this passage is powerful as it speaks to the implications of marriage. One scholar has said that this passage *characterizes marital love as the strongest, most unyielding and invincible force in human experience.*

Now that's saying something! Despite the failure of individuals, the bar of God's expectations for marriage is set sky-high. And note the implications of the last part of verse 7: True, lasting marital love involves deep integrity on the part of both parties. To paraphrase: *"Money can't buy me love"*.

The power of marriage lies in the power of a promise, sealed with God's stamp of approval, that one man makes to one woman. The promise to love another person "*until death do you part*" is as deep a commitment as one can make in this life.

As one pastor put it, "*The power to make and keep a promise is one of the strongest in the world, for it brings the promise maker within a millimeter of what it means to be like God, who makes and keeps his promises to his people.*"

True, enduring, lifelong commitment is God's expectation for marriage, and it has been since the Garden of Eden. That's not to say that God expects us to be perfect as we relate to one another; we are, after all, still living under the effects of sin. But despite our failures, the goal for the respect we are to show toward the institution remains the same, "*for love is as strong as death, its jealousy unyielding as the grave*".
So Robert, go on and be strong, you can do it!"

"Amen Rev. thank you"

"That's right Robert, and start saving for that rock_ Hahaha, alright let's move on to the next caller, DJ Mutoba on the line, who is this?"

"Hey fam. it's Jerome from Mississauga and my question to Rev. Al Bareck is what is the advice you have for us men in regards to a do-over?"

"Blessings to you Jerome, I will take you to the book of Joel 2:12–27. To kids on a playground, the concept of a "do-over" is well known. When they're playing kickball and the ball gets stuck in a tree, or when they're playing basketball and the ball sticks between the backboard and the rim, a chorus of "do over" spontaneously erupts. It's an unspoken rule that every kid knows.

Sometimes as adults we wish we could resurrect the rule in our own lives. When we miss a bill payment, we long to be able to appeal to the utility company for a "do-over." When we speak a thoughtless word that hurts another person, we wish for the same.

Through the prophet Joel God tells the Israelites they can have a "do-over." If they'll repent God will return what he has taken away in punishment. Apparently a plague of locusts has destroyed the nation's crops, and God promises to give the people abundant harvests once again.

So how can we make the reality of the "do-over" active in our life once again? Truth be told, this concept usually doesn't work in our adult lives and relationships without a good deal of work and humility on our part. We bear the consequences of our mistakes until regret grows and we ask for forgiveness.

That's when grace can intervene, and the person we've harmed can forgive. The same is true in our relationship with God. If we understand that sin has kept us from realizing our potential, we need to do the same as the Israelites: repent. In this case, we don't really achieve the "do-over" ourselves; instead, we receive it from God. We simply turn to God with our confession.

Many men find confession especially difficult because it cuts at our dignity and self-worth. When we confess we admit our mistakes and failures. We assume that these admissions don't make us look very good.

However, God loves to see us confess and repent of our sin, because in doing so we show that we desire to turn to him. When we're "*man enough*" to confess our wrongs, God can choose to pour out his blessings for the next phase of our lives."

"Woah, that was deep! And do you have any scriptures I can read through and all to build up on this?"

"Yep, give me a second here_go read the following Psalm 32:1–11; Ezekiel 33:10–16; and Acts 2:37–39"

"Thanks, God bless"

"No worries, Jerome that is why we're here, and before you go, which station just gave you the blaze you needed?"

"Yessir, Church-Vibe 84.4FM, that's how we do it with DJ Mutoba on the BlazoBlaze show! _ Hahaha"

"Yeah, yeah! I should have him join me as co-host_Toronto talk to me, this is your one and only DJ Mutoba and we are right here keeping it real in the Lord with Reverend Jeff Al Bareck also known as Rev. Al B._ Caller you are live on the air who's this?"

"Word! This is Matt from Mississauga and with a few guys here at the office we had a discussion about divorce, and then one of us said what God has joined together let no man temper with but how do you elaborate on that, I mean how real can it be?"

"Divorce, the devil is trying to gain serious ground with it, let's turn to Deuteronomy 24: 1-5 and dig deeper into this very important statement of *what God has joined together*.

Most of us would agree that divorce is not a laughing matter. But that doesn't stop people from joking about it, like one comedian who said, "My ex-wife is a great housekeeper—

when we got divorced, she kept the house." Legal terms like "no fault" and "uncontested" fuel the idea that divorce is an easy, acceptable alternative to marriage. Instead of treating divorce seriously, people begin to view it as just another option to be considered in the context of modern relationships.

Some people even look to the Bible to justify divorce. They search Scripture to find "loopholes" in God's rules for marriage. But we're missing the point when we hunt for God's permission to divorce.

For a deeper understanding of God's true perspective on marriage, we need to look at the provisions he extends to newlyweds in Deuteronomy 24:5. God excuses the recently married man from many responsibilities—including military service—for a full year so that he can give his full attention to his wife.

Think about that. God's gift to newlyweds was a whole year to work on building a solid foundation in their marriage. One year for the husband to learn to meet his wife's needs. One year to hone their communication skills. One year to prepare for life's journey together.

God clearly supports the institution of marriage. Throughout Scripture he offers invaluable help to husbands and wives who commit themselves to each other for life.

If you're married, think about this: What if you'd been given a year after your wedding to focus only on your wife? How would your relationship be different today?

It's not too late to find out. Maybe you don't have an entire year, but you can start with a day at a time. Clear your schedule so that you can give your wife your undivided attention.

If you have commitments that take you away from home on the evenings and weekends, consider dropping one or two of them to focus on your relationship. Listen to her concerns. Commit yourself to meeting her needs. Look for ways to bring her happiness. With God's help, you can turn your marriage into a love story for the ages."

"Ooooh! Ooooh!" sounds of cheers erupted in the background.

"Matt, is everything okay there?"

"Yes we are Rev. it's the rest of the guys listening to you on the radio, I guess it's clear and precise, God Bless!"

"Alright listeners we're going to take another break; when we come back I will read over 2 emails from our inbox and have Reverend Al Bareck respond to you. Then we shall go back to the phone lines but in the mean time, keep it locked on Church-Vibe 84.4 FM – Where the truth is not hidden but shared"

Nine

"Church-Vibe 84.4FM, this is the BlazoBlaze show and we are live in studio with Reverend Jeff Al Bareck. For those who just joined, we are addressing the topic of sexuality, divorce and relationships. How were all those things intended to be by the Highest God. We have an email here and it reads:

-We need help, our marriage is very shaky and at edge of divorce I must say. I work hard at work to provide for my family but I have the feeling my wife is having an affair. Doesn't the bible say that a man can repudiate his wife if she commits adultery? - Signed Rudolf_ So Rev, what is your say on that?"

"I don't like the word divorce. It's taking too much of our beautiful couples out there! It is important to note that
God is our refuge and strength, an ever-present help in trouble. Refer yourselves to Psalm 46:1–11.

Ask yourselves the question; what could shake the very foundation of your marriage?

I had a situation like that in my church, for the purpose of this example I will name them Rick and Sandy; it started with Rick's working too much. With each promotion, Rick spent more time on the road and less time with Sandy. But success at work left him empty.

He bought things he couldn't afford to reward himself for his long hours away. Soon he and Sandy were arguing over money.

To pay the mounting bills, Sandy found a job. She also found a sympathetic friend at work and tried to heal her hurts with an affair. When Rick found out about the affair, he quietly made plans to divorce Sandy.

Before the papers could be filed, however, Sandy got sick with a minor illness. But complications set in, and she was put into the hospital. More than once, the doctors told Rick that she wouldn't make it through the night.

That night Rick began to see things differently. He wanted to save the marriage, but he didn't know how. As Sandy's illness became progressively worse, she went into a coma. Rick feared for her life and spent every waking moment by her side.

In Psalm 46, we see the world being torn apart by cataclysmic disasters—mountains collapsing into the sea, earthquakes, floods and military conquests.

But the author of this psalm tells us that we shouldn't fear. How could we not be afraid when faced with such terrifying events?

The psalmist tells us that through all of the turbulence, God is with us. God is our refuge and strength when problems shake our world. He has such awesome power that the world actually melts at the sound of his voice. God is in control and will be exalted.

As Sandy lay in the hospital, fighting to live, Rick was fired from his job. He had to sell their house and their car. But when everything he thought was important was stripped away, Rick found God was there through it all. When he heard God's voice, it was as if his earthly troubles melted away. Rick believed God was in control and that Sandy would live. And she did.

Today Sandy is permanently disabled. She requires full-time care. Life will never be the same for this couple. But their marriage has withstood the worst threats possible. They now trust God daily for healing, forgiveness and the restoration of their marriage.

They endured past trials and found that God was their refuge. They will face future trials knowing he is their strength. Their marriage has never been stronger.

Whatever long, dark nights you face as a couple, let this passage remind you that God is ever-present, the morning will come, and the battle has already been won."

"Amen! Reverend, we pray for them and may the Lord be with them"

"Amen indeed"

"Reverend, I think the issue we have here is that when couples have a problem, it directly opens a route for division, what can you share with our listeners today, what should they do when trouble comes their way to divide them?"

"Glad you ask that DJ Mutoba, I will reference myself to Ecclesiastes 12 vs. 1 to 14 and it reads,

Remember your Creator in the days of your youth, before the days of trouble come and the years approach when you will say, "I find no pleasure in them.

You see, there are days—sometimes many of them—when it is hard to remember what it was about your spouse that you once found so lovable. Most of us expect a few waves on the voyage to marital bliss. We might even find humor in our spouse's foibles and failings. But what happens when those waves swell into crushing tsunamis?

What do we do when a spouse falls into a depression, when infertility becomes the only topic of conversation, or when one of us loses a job?

Take for example my assistant, in her first year of marriage, her husband who is a teacher walked into a war zone. He taught fourth-grade boys with severe emotional and behavioral problems.

Between their physical aggression, verbal hostility and profound inability to control their inappropriate behavior, these young boys sucked the spirit out of her husband. He would come home exhausted, unable to offer the family much of anything.

For the first few months, she remained sympathetic. But as the year went on, she came to resent his job—and his desire to do it—for the toll it was taking on their relationship and their children.

That year she lived with Dave at his worst—his most depressed, most damaged, most disillusioned self. There were days when she truly wondered if she could sustain their marriage with him doing that kind of work.

Yet in the midst of all this awfulness, God kept showing her the things she loved about Dave: his heart for broken people, his strength of character, his resilience and tenderness.

It would have been easy for her to miss the good Dave was trying to accomplish because of the overwhelming nature of the bad it brought with it. It certainly wasn't her strength that kept their family together during that time; it was God's.

Look carefully at Ecclesiastes 12:1. It doesn't say, "*Remember your Creator just in case the days of trouble come.*" It says *trouble will come. It comes to everyone sooner or later.* That's not a reason to despair but a reason to shore up our reserves. Like a cruise ship equipped with lifeboats, we need to be prepared for the hard times by treasuring the good.

So spend some time remembering your dating days. Flip through the photos from your honeymoon. Tell each other what you admire about each other and why that will never change. Then, when trouble comes, you'll have a trustworthy life raft to hold you up as you make your way to the calm shore on the other side."

"Thank you Reverend, we are just going to take one call here_caller you are live?"

"Thank you DJ Mutoba, morning Rev. My name is Angela and I am suspecting my fiancé of having an affair but what puzzles me is that he is very involved in church. Is a fidelity check a wrong approach?"

As this lady finished her words, on the other side of town, Karen, Val and Mirella stayed speechless in front of the radio and awaited the response of the Rev.

"Let me ask you this Angela, you have suspected that and what have you done in regards to that so far?"

"Well, my antennas went up_ I am watching for evidence such as receipts, phone calls, emails, tweets to confirm my suspicion."

"And is it clear now that he is actually cheating?"

"Yes, he is"

"Have you confronted him on that?"

"I surely did and he said I was crazy for thinking that way. His words cut me to the core. Not only did his vehement denial magnify his guilt, but also his demeaning words reinforced what I was already feeling—that I am losing my mind. Jealousy and more suspicion is taking over my life, I need help"

"My dear sister, at some point, every couple will experience feelings of jealousy and suspicion. While we might not have a modern-day equivalent to the bitter-water litmus test of Numbers 5:11–31, there are some practical steps we can take to deal with fears of infidelity and to restore trust once it has been broken by an affair.

For starters, we can pray daily for a hedge of protection around our union. Jerry Jenkins explains how this works in his book Hedges (Good News/Crossway, 2005).

Second, we can build a climate of trust with our partner through open communication and checkpoints that give our partner windows into our world. Without allowing it to become controlling, there's nothing wrong with setting up checkpoints that verify our whereabouts, our communications with others, and what we do when we're alone.

I do however strongly encourage you to take this to the Pastor and elders in your church. This is not a small matter that can be dealt with in one day. If you know the woman, call her up and ask her to come to the church too. She probably doesn't even know Christ, just like she might be a fervent praying woman too! But remember that the Lord shall never let you down no matter the circumstance. "

"Alright, I will try"

"Val, did you hear that, I think Chantel should go and talk to Angela and tell her the truth the way she told us."

"You know Karen, I agree with you on that one. It's important; this is a very serious matter."

Ten

"Chantel, the girls and I were wondering if we could all meet and have a real talk."

"A real talk, hmm, sure, you guys wanna come to my place?"

"Okay, I will pick up Karen, Mirella and Val"

Considering the traffic on highway 401, it took the girls a good three hours before they could reach the 101 Erskine.

The group was nervous, they were not sure if their long time friend was going to kindly ask them to depart from her property after the talk or if she was going to go with the flow.

"Hey, we are finally downstairs" Val said with a tired voice.

"It's about time girls, I almost called the cops to track you guys down" Chantel responded jokingly as she buzzed them in.

"I love this place, I heard she even has concierge service "

"Really, hmm, neat, next time she goes on vacation I am moving in here Hahaha"

"Knock knock, is anyone home"

"Just come in, the door is open girls"

Startling get together as usual, a Dom Pérignon Oenothèque for the girls, a few hors d'oeuvre and as usual Chantel welcomes her guests in grandeur!

"So, I'm listening, what is it that brings the big five to a meeting on this day?"

"Well_ Karen, Val and I had been listening to the radio the other day and there was this show on Church-Vibe 84.4 about relationships and all_"

"Oh neat, I never heard of that station, I should check it out someday"

"Yeah, you should, they got some good southern gospel on it, modern Christian too and a talk-show that we followed which brings us here."

"Okay Karen, just before you go any further girl, I am not investing in a radio station, been there and not doing it anymore."

"No Chantel, it's more serious than that. It's in regards to the Ryan dude"

"_Oh, him again, what did he do this time? To whom did he lie?"

"Yep, he is under the radar again but this time he's been challenged by his fiancé; she suspects he cheated and apparently you are not the only one with whom he did it"

"My, my, my, you are kidding me girl_ and how do you guys know that?"

"Well, she called on the radio show"

"She who? His fiancé_ girl are you pulling my leg or something because if that's the case, just take my Louboutin shoes and we good for this one!"

"I will take the shoes alright! But no, it's that serious, she called in during the show and the guy denied having an affair or affairs"

"This is unreal, I can't believe that guy, and are you also trying to tell me that they are still engaged as we speak?"

"Sadly girl they are still engaged and who knows what is next"

"That is unfortunate, why don't you guys tell her it's high time she left him!"

"Exactly why we came here, we were wondering if_"

"Noo, Nooo, Noooo girl, are you out of your mind, you want me to go in front of the girl and say – hey, I had a one night stand with your man and euh, by the way he never said he was engaged but I think you should dump him! Girl, just tell her to play him back."

"Well, not really in those words but you kinda grasp the entire concept"

"Girls, I understand the concern and all, but I am not going to go meet her. I already felt ashamed when you guys told me that the dude was engaged and now you want me to go again and pause in front of the girl! Nope, it's not happening"

"Okay, so what do you think is reasonable?"

"_In all honesty, Karen you are the best placed person. You know her, Ryan and me. Meaning only you can help shade some light. It's not like you are snooping on anyone; because for her to talk about it live on radio, girl it's got to be serious!"

"Fair enough, would you come with me like a moral support type of thing?"

"Karen, I don't think I can face her, I can wait for you in the car if I drive you there; _why do you guys want me to meet her anyway? Is there something I am missing or something you guys are not saying?"

"Chantel, it is complicated, very complicated."
"Let's put our brains together here and break it down, Val you're good at that!"

"I need food before that"

"Val, are you kidding us right now?" the rest of the girls exclaimed as they shook their heads. Despite the ignorance the other girls gave, Val was not being cooperative and insisted on being fed before she could give them what she called rescue 101. Chantel finally gave in and had the concierge service take care of the dinner.

"Alright ladies, let's get down to business, I am well fed and energized to break it down to you."

"Preach on, it's about time!"

"First, this entire idea of having Chantel call Angela, don't make sense in the entire world and in all the billion languages available on earth!"

"Aha_told you it was not a good idea for me to talk to the girl!"

"Excuse me, I'm talking ladies_ next, Karen, you know both Ryan and Angela. You heard Angela on Church-Vibe, so you call up the sister, drop it to her that you heard the show that day and give her your supporting shoulder; from that point, you can tell her that after the show, a girl you know told you she knows the guy and he does not even mention of his commitment to her.

Then if she asks to meet with Chantel we shall figure something out, if she cool with what she hears then it's up to her to decide if she is giving back the rock to the giver or if she is giving him another chance after she takes him to rehab!"

"Dang! Val nailed it again, our one and only Psychologist Hahaha"

"That's what I'm talking about ladies, and when you do it that way, Angela is still your friend and it does not bring unnecessary tension."

"True, I like that vibe, I am seeing her tomorrow."

"How is that?"

"Well she's the owner of the new women's fitness club near union station, and she hired my firm for her PR stuff, so we are having lunch together tomorrow."

"Okay, too much info for now, Chantel, thank you for the hospitality, we've been well hospitalized during these few or should I say numerous hours?"

"Val, Val, Val, what will I do without you? _ But you are welcome girl and see you guys tomorrow"

"Bye girl" Val, Karen and Mirella enthusiastically responded as Chantel closed the door behind them.

Eleven

"Thanks for joining me for lunch Karen; I really need some girl time right now."

"No worries, that's what friends are for, I don't mean to be indiscreet or anything but I heard you on the BalzoBlaze show the other day"

"It's okay girl, that's how bad it is, if I can even talk about it on the radio, that's how much I regret the entire thing right now_ I need some serious help. I don't know what to do or where to start."

"Aww, don't worry girl. Things will work out; you know when you start saying if only we hadn't gotten engaged, married so soon. If only we had more money. If only I had gone for Jason instead of Ryan. Regrets in relationships are damaging.

They keep our eyes fixed on the rearview mirror instead of on the road ahead. While reviewing the past and assessing what we've learned through mistakes can be a healthy exercise, regretting the past only serves to fuel discontentment and impede growth.

When Martin and I decided to close a three-year-old business, I struggled with regret. I had used up all of our nest egg to pursue a business venture I had believed in. When the business failed, I regretted so many decisions I had made, especially not listening to Martin's advice along the way.

My failure meant that we would be struggling financially again after having enjoyed several years of monetary comfort. Even though I knew God had walked us through this difficult time and taught us invaluable lessons, it was tempting to think, "If I hadn't tried to start that new business, we'd be financially set right now." Instead of keeping my eyes focused on God's plan for my life, I chose to get stuck in my tracks with if-only thinking.

"I hear you Karen, but it's hard and we are almost married, all that is left is the religious ceremony, we have finished paying almost everything."

"I know, look at Lot's wife, she had a similar problem. She and her husband were running for their lives from Sodom and Gomorrah, knowing that God had judged the culture they were living in and was about to decimate everything they had ever known.

While Lot was running full steam ahead, his wife kept looking over her shoulder. Eventually, the distance between them became so great that Lot literally left his wife in the dust.

Regret is like that. We keep looking over our shoulder, wondering if what we've left behind might have been better than what we're moving toward. God's angel warned Lot and his wife not to look back, and it's a warning for us too."

"So are you saying I should forget what he did to me, and continue with this relationship?"

"What I am saying is if you routinely catch yourself starting a sentence with "If only," regret may be an issue you need to deal with. While dwelling on what might have been is never healthy, regret can be an important signal to stop and examine your emotions.

For instance, if you catch yourself thinking, "If only I had married Jason instead of Ryan," it may be time to evaluate why Ryan isn't measuring up. In your private time with God, pray about the emotions you're experiencing.

Perhaps you'll discover that your disappointment is springing from unmet needs. With these needs clarified, you can then have a forward-thinking conversation with Ryan about how to improve your relationship. When I caught myself saying, "If only I hadn't tried to start this business," I realized that my fear of God's inability to meet our needs in the future was driving my regret.

Once I discovered that, I could stop looking to the past and begin focusing on a vision for what God might accomplish in our future. It's going to be fine Angela."

"I don't know where I will find the strength to go through this, if at least he could admit that he cheated, that would help but he's not accepting."

"On that one, I'd ask him again calmly, if he denies then tell me. We shall evolve from there_ is that fair enough?"

"_I guess it is, Karen, I don't even know if I want to be who I am anymore, it's hard. I am so confused right now."

"It's going to be fine girl, God's got your back and front"

"Can you do me a favor Karen?"

"Sure girl, if I can, I will and if I can't we shall find someone who can_ how about that?"

"Fair, can you talk to Ryan for me?"

"_You want me to talk to Ryan_ euh, about this entire thing?"

"Yes, could you?"

"Okay, I will, as a matter of fact, let me drive up to his workplace, I will talk to him. Go get some rest at home_okay"

"Thanks girl, I really appreciate"

"No worries"

Puzzled with the favour her friend had just asked, she drove off to meet Chantel and recap on what had just happened. The two girls agreed to drive down and meet Ryan and shake some silliness out of him.

"Ryan!"

"Hey, Karen how you doing? What brings you here?"

"I am well and you bring me here, we need to talk!"

"Okay, that doesn't sound good, when you come here and say that, I know there is trouble somewhere, close the door behind you and take a seat let's get down to business."

"Ryan, I am from meeting up with Angela, and I must say, I am not impressed with how you are treating her right now_ you begged me to hook you guys up and that you'd be faithful to her and treat her well, but that is not what I am hearing or seeing, so explain Mr."

"Karen, calm down, I guess we had an argument and that's it. It's all good. I am faithful to her."

"Ryan, don't push it. You know me better."

"Push you how? For crying out loud! And how you go' come in my office and accuse me of stuff!"

"Really! Give me a second." Karen reached for her purse and took her phone "Allo, yeah, come in the office I entered."

"Is that Angela?"

"No Ryan, it's not" and as the door opened with gentleness, Chantel walked in and sat next to her friend Karen and shook her head as she looked at Ryan.

"You guys know each other?" Ryan asked taken aback.

"We don't know each other, we are Sisters Ryan, Karen and I go way back to elementary school. And I must say, I am saddened to see that you go around town lying that you are a single man, meanwhile you've had the audacity of proposing to one of our girls, and to make matters worse, you pride yourself to be a serving man of God yet your behavior is a reflection of a Jezebel men version! What wrong did Angela do you for you to go around doing such a ghastly thing?"

"Girls, I don't know, I know I really messed up_ And I denying the entire thing does not help. I just couldn't take it anymore. My business is shutting down, I am at the verge of bankruptcy, the pastor doesn't have time to listen, he is always busy, and Angela was too busy focusing on her gym project.

As much as I was showing resentment, it did not seem to bother her much; I expected more from her but I was not getting anything. I then decided to play around and unfortunately it ended up into this big jumble."

"Ryan_ seriously, you know you can always come to me for advice. And here you are fooling around with Chantel, yet she is the most efficient person at restructuring small businesses_ but why are you denying your affairs?"

"Karen, Chantel, it's not as easy as you think, she even went on live radio to talk about this! How do you think my employees perceive me?

That is the only station that plays in the workshop and they were all there hearing the boss's future wife pouring her heart to the city!"

"Ryan, when Angela confronted you, why did you deny?"

"Why? _ don't be silly, I wasn't just going to seat there and admit it!"
"Ryan, so what do you want to do now?"

"I don't know, it's not me, I don't know, I handed in my resignation at the church too. I am shaken by own acts."

"Ryan, unlike you, Karen and Angela, I am not a church person, but there is one thing I know and that is marriage binds husband and wife into a unity that changes both of them.

While individual identities shouldn't be crushed as "two become one," it is also true that we cannot remain isolated or independent from one another. But in the fusing that takes place, both good and bad things can happen.

When we share our lives well, we can strengthen our mate's resolve, nurture our spouse's well being and encourage each other's gifts. Unfortunately, we can also have a negative impact on each other. We can entice our partner into supporting our mistakes and sins.

We can ask our spouse to cover up for us when the phone rings and we don't wish to be found. We can lie for our mate in public settings. We can manipulate our spouse into falsifying tax returns or hiding assets.

Marriage makes us complicit in the morality of our mate. That is an important reason to choose wisely before we wed and to build upon a strong moral center in our relationship after we are joined.

Great businesses don't collapse overnight through some minor accounting error; their foundations slowly erode as leaders make each other complicit in deceptive schemes.

So it is in marriages. While we can win for a while as we help each other cheat on the truth, in the long run we build a kingdom of facades in which we can neither trust our partner's face nor clearly see our own.

On the other hand, when we learn from mistakes like those of I think the name is Jeroboam and his wife in the bible; we can build a complicity of goodness that our children and friends will admire someday when they help us celebrate our silver and golden wedding anniversaries!

You are a good man, she is a good woman too, and God is always good. Don't destroy but maintain and continue building what you have started."

"It's easy to say Chantel, its easy_"

"And it is hard to do Ryan, but it's easy to try"

"Come on Ryan, you know better that the success of a marriage comes, not in finding who we think initially is the "perfect" person for us, but in our willingness to adjust to the real person we married. "

"True, true."

"When you saw all that happening, why didn't you call an immediate cease fire?"

"I tried but everyone around me was too busy, and when I went out on two different dates, I found comfort that Angela had withheld from me, do you realize that this is since last year!"

"I am sorry to hear that. I know it hurts, but trust me, Angela loves you, she is just a bit confused with everything and after speaking with her, she does not even know that she is the one who triggered that. You might want to talk to her and tell her the truth the way it is."

"Do you know Angela too?"

"No, I have never met her, I only heard of her when I told Karen about you."

"Okay, I hear you_ well, I hope you forgive me Chantel for the lie and the lack of respect I have shown you in behaving myself in that manner."

"Apology accepted and forgiven, we shall put up a plan to get your business back on its feet"

"Thank you, but that will be subject to Angela's approval, you know what I mean"

"Totally fine by me"

"Karen, I hope you find a place in your heart to forgive me. I deceived you in many ways, hurting your friends Angela and Chantel, lying to you. I truly do hope that you find that place.

I know things might never be the same again between us but as long as we all go our ways without hating each other, I'd appreciate that a lot, you have no idea. If Angela decides to end it, I am responsible for that and I will have to endure the consequences of my misbehavior_"

"Ryan, it is true, but don't worry about me for now.

Focus on your relationship. There is this guy, Ernest Boyer, he said, "Marriage is a most remarkable and courageous human act," "It's the promise of two human beings to share life together on all levels, physical, economic, and spiritual.

It's a promise made despite the certainty of death, the certainty of change, and the uncertainty of everything else. There is nothing else we might choose to do that is quite like this act, nothing so foolish or so profound."

"Yep, I wonder why so many of us enter into this "foolish and profound" commitment when we realize that it is such a difficult thing to unify two separate individuals? Why do we assume we will have success when we know that others fail?"

"Ryan, before his death, David shared his vision for building a temple for the Lord with his son Solomon, to whom God had entrusted this sacred task. David had spent countless hours collecting and preparing all of the materials his son would need to build a house worthy of the Lord.

Then David told Solomon that if he was careful to observe the laws of the Lord, he would have success. Likewise we, too, need to take great care in preparing for the construction of a marriage. Marriage is like a temple—a magnificent living, breathing house for the Lord. When we stand at the altar exchanging wedding vows, we're essentially agreeing to erect a temple in which to honor God. By following God's plan for marriage—loving, honoring, and remaining faithful to each other—we will have success in honoring him. When we're strong and courageous, we'll be able to overcome obstacles and persevere."

"True, and that is exactly what I failed to do_ I failed to be loving, honoring and remain faithful to Angela"

"It sounds easy. But it's not. When Martin and I were preparing to get married, we spent an entire year budgeting, envisioning, and getting quotes on bands, caterers, cakes and invitations—planning all of the elements that go into making a wedding day a success.

Soon after we walked down the aisle as Mr. and Mrs., we realized we would need to apply that same kind of care to building our relationship for a lifetime, not just planning for a day.

Marriages often include struggles. Changes in career aspirations, guilt feelings over past mistakes, conflicts in other relationships—these and a myriad of other situations present many opportunities to be either the afflicted or the comforter within marriage. In these periods the one doing the supporting may begin to think, "I am not being helped by this person, only held back." But because of that foolish, extraordinary vow of marriage, he or she keeps going."

"Are you sure, you don't want to work for ministry Karen?"

"Shut up Chantel_ So, Ryan as I was saying, through the ordinary pains and sharing of day-to-day life, marital love matures into a love that models God's own love for us. It is in this temple we call marriage that God profoundly manifests himself; giving us the tools we need to be successful as husband and wife."

"Thank you Karen, if you never ever go to church again, I take account of that for my wrong doings. Chantel, I hope I did not mess up your reputation, and if someone ever doubts of your true version, you can send him or her my way.

Today is a hard day for me, I have to tell my employees that in two months we might shut down unless otherwise. I will try and approach Angela on this, and I guess see where the talk takes us.

I appreciate you looking out for Angela and for me, it seems you guys want this thing to work and don't get me wrong I am in the same vibe but I guess I need to understand that when something is Forbidden, it is Forbidden for a reason and also that when a wrong is caused it is not Forbidden to talk of it because withholding it will only destroy self more."

"You will be okay Ryan, take it slowly. Don't worry about your employees for now, worry about your household."

"Thank you Karen"

"Anytime"

"Well, at least now you know that a secret is not really a secret because sooner or later…it will come up, you can run but you can't hide!"

"True, give me a second, I just got to make a quick call"

"Oh sure, go ahead, we're going to get going too anyway_"

"Yeup, it won't be five minutes, I will walk you guys out. _ Allo, babe, it's me Ryan, can we meet at Marcel's in an hour or so?"

"Sure, is everything okay, you sound terrible?"

"I'm okay_guess tired, I will see you there. Bye"

Twelve

"Alright ladies, I guess we are calling it a wrap from here. Thank you again for your time and enjoy the rest of your day."

"Be good dear" Chantel and Karen responded as they began to walk towards the exit of the shop.

Ryan stayed back to pack his documents and send a few emails. The time came, he took his car and off he was on his way to Marcel's to meet up with Angela.

"Welcome to Marcel's are you meeting a party or you would like a table for yourself?"

"Actually yeah, table for two, my lady should be here in a minute or two, just write Ryan_ she will ask for me once she reaches."

"Certainly sir, please follow Kim, she will direct you to your table"

"Thank you"

A few minutes elapsed and Kim was bringing Angela to the table too.

"Hey Babe, how are you?"

"I'm good, how is it going at the gym?"

"It's going well, I just managed to get a deal with two companies in the building where I am, so exited"

"Congrats to you dear, keep on pushing and before you know it, you will be located at the four corners of the city."

"Hmm, that will be good but I would prefer that type of expansion at least after 2 years of dominance where we are located."

"_Let me ask you this, from business school do you think that those principles are helping in leading your business venture?"

"In a way yes they are, but I wish I had followed your advise of doing some of it online because then I'd be working on my project while in school instead of focusing on it after school_ how are things at the shop?"

"Things are going very slow actually. I have lost most of my accounts and I might be going out next month."

"Going out_ as in closing?"

"Yes Angela, it's the end of my venture; to make things more simple, I am bankrupt."

"You are what? _ When did this happen?"

"You heard me right, bankrupt, I lost major accounts. Yellow Cab and Blue line taxi have their own repair shops now. Toronto police has not renewed their contract either, Hamilton police neither. I only have Peel-Regional police so far but it's not enough to keep me running."

"Ryan_ why didn't you tell me that all this was happening at the shop?"

"I did, but you were too caught up in your own world, I asked the pastor too but he was too busy, there was no one to turn to and these things kept on pushing me to the extreme. I even started drinking again_"

"Ryan, you are acting like I am not your wife to be?"

"I am acting to the result of you not giving time for us, we don't talk about us no more, we only talk about our problems."

"Is that so_ we only talk about our problems, you are the one who doesn't give me time!"

"I am the one, who follows you at work, I am the one who emails you because you can't be long on the phone_ running to a meeting babe, catch you in a bit_ I am the one who is always on time for all these appointments we have with the wedding planer... what else is a man to do? Tell me Angela?"

"Ryan I can explain, I didn't mean for it to come out that way but you have been acting strange for the past few months_"

"That is an under statement, I have been acting very strange, do you want to go continue this conversation at my place or your place?"

"Sure, we can go to my place since it's closer."

The couple stood and together walked out of the restaurant hand in hand. Something they had not done for a few months. Angela and Ryan met through Karen. It was at a franchise show that the two were introduced and Ryan could not get his mind off Angela from that day on.

He insisted that Karen work up something so he could get to meet her again and then see how he could hook up with her, she swept him off his foot as the temptations say it.

Karen was no easy person to convince, her considering Ryan as a brother and Angela as a good friend, she did not want to ruin any relation she had with the two but eventually succumbed to the pressure of her pal.

The two began to date and eventually got engaged two years later; but as they were in the final phase of the wedding preparations, is where most of the challenges occurred.

"Do you want anything to drink?"

"Sure a coffee would be good."

"Coffee, you drink coffee too now? Ryan! I am giving you hot chocolate"

"Sure, as long as it's warm, I'm good"

"Give me a few minutes, I will be right back"

"Take your time, I got all day."

"Okay, so tell me more, what's happening with this entire bankruptcy, personality change, we can not start our married life in that route Ryan"

"True, the shop thing, it is what it is, I had a few meetings with my major accounts and hopefully they respond in my favour. However I have to ask for your forgiveness_ a few weeks ago, you confronted me on whether I had or whether I was having an affair on the side.

The crew and I at the shop also heard you when you called the BlazoBlaze show and literally poured your heart. Well, I did have two aff_"

"You had two affairs! Are you kidding me! Two affairs!"

Angela screamed as she began to walk back and forth in the living room looking at him with angry eyes that could light up the place in fire.

"Angela, be calm and listen to me"

"Ryan, you expect me to seat here and say good job!" she screamed back as she walked to the kitchen and back to the leaving room with a tissue box in her hand.

"No, I expect you to seat down and look back and ask yourself how we got to that_how can we be arguing about such a huge thing a few months away from our wedding_"

"But_ all these days you kept on denying when I'd ask_ you told me I was stress_"

"Stressing, yes. You were stressing and you took us into it. Angie, I am not here to blame you over stuff but I am here to ask for forgiveness, will you hear me out?"

"_Fine, shoot" she answered back as she took off her engagement ring, placing it on the coffee table.

"As_ as I was saying, I am sorry for the wrong I have done you. You noticed something was wrong and you came to see me. I lied to you, I had two dates, one of them we had a drink and spoke a lot about life in general. The other one, was a night out, we drunk lots and then unfortunately it ended too far. The thi_"

"Too far as in what? Too far as in sex?" no need to hide now Ryan" Angela furiously interrupted and looking straight ahead in front of her.

"Yes, that is where it ended. The thing is, you were too busy for me. Yet, when I went on my first date, she did not know I was engaged but she showed me who indeed I was. She understood me. I told her I had problems with my girl friend and we spoke more"

"Wow, from fiancée to girl friend, you amaze me Ryan, carry on, I am listening, and the second date, what was I? Your ex?"

"Angie please, calm down, let me break it down to you. The second date, I went drinking. It's the day I asked you out on a date, you cancelled on me 30 minutes before our date and all you gave me for excuse was that you had a long day and was too tired, I even asked if I could come and meet you here so we could spend some time together but you seemed too busy to meet up with me_me your husband to be"

"It's not that Ryan, it's not that, I was_I don't even know how to explain, I was wrong yes but is that a motive to go ahead and sleep with another woman? And on top of that you are an assistant pastor! Ryan why would you do that?"

"Angela, I am a man. You and I started growing apart. I was missing my woman. I tried all I could to keep you near me but it seemed you were pushing me away. Usually, you'd come to my shop and check up on the boys and me, but it had been a few months that you never showed up, neither for coffee nor for close_ your check up phone calls became rare and your person in me became absent if not a stranger!"

"Ryan, why and how could you_ I don't even know what to do right now. I don't even know if we should get married anymore, you are already cheating on me and _oh my, I don't know what _what to say."

"It's okay, I understand you. I have already sent my resignation at the church. That position is not mine. I told the pastor of my acts too and he said he'd get back to me in a few days. Now I am talking to you. My intention was not to hurt you or me, or the other girls. I felt abandoned. I was not even able to pray my way out of it. I begged you, looking for you all over the city_ ANGIE! You are my wife for crying out loud! And today, I am here with this problem but you are still acting selfish towards me"

"SELFISH! SELFISH! You better chose your words right before I pack you up with everything you ever gave me."

"Angela, you are more than a fiancée and more than a wife to be for me, but if you don't want to go on with us, it's okay I will understand."

"Ryan, I don't know what to tell you but I am going to ask you to leave for now."

"I understand, text or call me when you are ready to talk."

Ryan stood, caressed her shoulder as he passed by her and closed the door behind him.

"Allo Kar_Karen, its me Angela"

"Hey girl why are you crying?"

"Karen, Karen, why is this happening to me, Karen, I don't want anything to do with life no more, it's too much for me"

"Angela, it's going to be fine. Is it Ryan?"

"Yes, he had_Karen what am I to do?"

"You got to pray about it and take a decision. I cannot make you take a decision. I will respect your decision no matter what it is."

"Okay, I will, I will try, bye."

"Bye dear, call your mum too and see what she says"

"I can't, I don't even know how to start explaining to her. She is mum but we have never sat down and spoken on how I am to be in my marriage, how am I to take care of my fiancé, my husband, never, I don't know who to turn to now_ I feel lost and abandoned right now. I love Ryan and don't want to lose him."

"Can you forgive him and forget or forgive and remind him of his mistake every time he wont give you what you want?"

"Karen girl, as much as he is not blaming me or pointing his finger at me, I have a big part in it. I wanted to succeed so much with my business, that even my marriage's success was not a priority anymore and I guess I am paying the price right now."

"Come on girl, don't say that. Do as your heart says as long as your conscience is at ease. Have you spoken to Ryan since you last saw each other?"

"No, he left me a voicemail but I was unable to respond. I have to call him before its too late."

"Okay, do so and call me if you need anything"

She disconnected the call with her friend, took a breather and went back on the phone.

"Allo Ryan, its me"

"Hey dear, how doing?"

"I am a bit better, Ryan, I have been doing lots of think_ and it's not easy for me. I miss the good and bad times we've had in the pass. It's bad enough for me that I do not have any siblings to whom I can run and ask for help but I don't even have my man to whom I'd always run to.

I went to God in prayer and it has not been easy to pray out this situation we are having. I have loved you with all my heart and you know its true_ I feel lost, It is like I betrayed both you and me because I was not there for you when things were going upside down in your world and I was too self centered trying to establish myself and forgetting that I had something worth more than money"

"I know you loved me, I know we betrayed each other too."

Thirteen

"Evening ladies!"

"Mirella, how you doing girl, you disappeared since last time?"

"Your funny, I told you guys I was going with work to Calgary for the week, I just flew in yesterday"

"Oh yeah, I forgot, how was it?" Val responded as she continued drinking her wine.

"It went as usual, long meetings and blah_ anyway what did I miss while I was away? Any hot gossip on the frying pan?"

"Well, gossip is not the term this time; DRAM-DRAM-DRAMA is the term! With Karen and Chantel in the headlines!"

"Okay, we have a problem, because when angel Karen is involved, it means it is serious.

Girls start talking I am listening! Why didn't you Face time me or something?" Mirella said as she was lowering the volume of the television set.

"Chantel do the honors, I don't know where to start girl"

"Sure Karen, since I started the heat in their relation, I might as well. Okay, so remember that dude Ryan I had a fling with few weeks ago?"

"Yeah, yeah, the one Karen said he was some assistant pastor or something like?"

"Ain't you got some memory? Well, things got out of shape to the point that his fiancée called some radio show_"

"The BlazoBlaze show" the rest of girls interrupted in laughter

"Yeah, that shows! I've never heard of it_ but anyway, so she called and poured her heart live on the air"

"You are kidding me girl! So she called and said she knows her man had an aff_"

"Not an affair but affairs" Val responded again in laughter

"Val come on!" Karen interrupted "that wine is getting to you, Mirella; the girl noticed he was having an affair or two, so she confronted him and he denied the whole thing. Then after that she told me of it_"

"Oh yeah true, you guys know each other and how is that campaign you doing for her coming up?"

"It's going well_ but yeah, so then she asked me to go talk to Ryan since I know him from way back too, so I went with Chantel_"

"You girls are nuts! You went to his spot and what?"

"And I confronted him, he denied the thing but then I called Chantel in and he was literally stunt and confessed his forbidden maneuver!"

"Maneuver she says! Karen you are so funny."

"Well, what you guys did was good, I hope they are sorting out their problems, because when he and I went for a drink the guy was literally sobbing the entire evening."

"Wait a minute; you went for a drink with him? When did this happen?"

"I am friends with him, our limo fleet gets serviced at his shop but then one evening he asked me out for a drink, no strings attached because he wanted an insight on how to start up an executive limo fleet, so we went out. All he spoke of was about his girl acting up_ why do you think I was stunt when Chantel went all the way to his bed!"

"Wow, Mirella that is so wrong, I did not go all the way to his bed, it happened and I have put it behind me. I don't need to be reminded that I slept with another girls man who is almost killing herself!"

"Sorry, but you need to be told that you do not sleep around with men as if you are a Marshal's opening for business or something!"

"Girls, girls, keep it down now, we are not here to judge, we are here to help!"

"I am calm Sheila, but if no one tells her the truth she won't know. Now Karen I do not mean to be rude, I know that out of all of us you are the church girl but despite me not being a church girl, I ain't got no time to bed hop and then when comes the time to get married my potential husband tells me no because I slept with his cousin or his boss or his best friend in the past!"

"Mirella, it's fine, I heard your point. I am a grown up woman but I appreciate you looking out for me. I messed up and I am not going that route anymore."

Chantel Responded as Val interrupted jokingly saying_ Confess girl, confess!

"Chantel, to add on to what Mirella is saying and this goes to all of us; bed hoping can take you to your grave with all these diseases that run around! So please be careful ladies, it sucks to be single but it's a plus to be healthy and knowing that you will be able to see your kids grow up healthy and your grand kids is a definite plus!"

"I am careful. I honestly don't know what got into me that night. I had vowed myself not to bed hop and it was going fine but there was something that just messed it up"

"Hmm, blame it on the alcohol girl! It works all the time," Val said as she continued laughing and pouring more wine in her glass.

"Val, stop being a hater for once, she is hurting and you are not helping_is that how you are going to be some preachers wife?"

"Karen, a preacher's wife has to say thing the way they are, not bit around the bush but on target! _ I'm just playing with you but I agree, it's important to take this seriously, too many diseases that are not written on the person's forehead nor on their bank card for that matter!"

"Here we go again she had to put the money in it" Mirella said as she poured herself a glass of wine and continued to interact with Karen "and do we know what they have concluded, are they still getting married or what are they doing?"

"Well, I don't know, neither has called me, so I guess they are still sorting it out"

"Well, all I got to say is, the ratio is 5:1 so stay healthy and don't mess up when you find thee one!" Sheila replied

"Cheers and amen to that_ Hahaha"

"VAL!!! How many glasses or bottles have you had since you got back from work?"

Fourteen

"Ryan, it is not easy for me, I don't know why we have to go through this" Angela continued as she was sniffing her tears.

"Angela, I was wrong_ I know and I admit. Instead of looking for comfort in alcohol and cigarettes, I should have gone to the Lord."

"Ryan_ all that is good but look at where we are today, I mean I could have said another name on radio, but I was so confused that I said it all_"

"It's okay dear, if I had opened up the first time you asked_ we were not going to end up there. I am equally responsible of this. I know you wanted your business to succeed but you forgot the main backbone of your business and we both forgot the main backbone of our union"

"Ryan, it's too hard for me, I am hurting like you have no idea, I don't know if I will be able to forget what happened_ it's too much for me to handle. I know I was to put God first but this is way more than punishment, how are the girls in the choir going to look at me? How will I stand in front and sing_ I just can't no more_ I don't think I can continue the entire thing of you and me being us"

In silence Ryan stood next to the window with his restless sight as Angela was pouring her heart away. He was there, looking at her, just a few meters apart from the one he once held dearly in his arms. A mere sight of compassion she did not even offer him as she focused towards the other side of the room.

Sadly he was accordingly dressed for the occasion, had his black suit, black shirt and necktie on, nicely groomed for a morose farewell that was awarded to him for his actions that he only did due to lack of attention from the one he loved.

The warm and cozy atmosphere he always enjoyed in the condo of his dear beloved was no more; it was consumed by an overwhelming emptiness that would not spare a single human to go into deep reflection.

And again he remembered how he saw the sunrise and sunset from that very window; yet still his heart, soul and mind were…if and only if, then that that is, his intelligence wondered.

Was it another cliché that his being was to face or was it the destiny that his footsteps heard of yet never cried of, for in a dungeon his heart, soul and mind were entering.

Speechless he remained, for all he would say even if given the opportunity by the mayor or the premier would be "I got no words". Most would say, you better have no words and others would look at him and understand what he was going through.

In silence, he stood for speechless was not the word, devastation could not sweep him off his feet, but yet leave him in silence for his heart, soul and mind were collapsing like the walls of Sodom and Gomorra.

Why, why, why, his intelligence wondered, confronted and yet the only remedy was yet to come. For the love of a woman, his heart thought it should cry...for the love of a God above all Gods, his soul was crying and whispering... he knew and felt... For the trials and tribulations, his mind was rotating, as a tornado would fiercely do.

Those eyes that once sparked the light at the end of the tunnel, no more blazes could they unveil as all they had were tears of sorrow. Tears that would still caress her cheeks and remind a confused mind that warmth could still be found somewhere, somehow, for some but not for all!

Sunrise after sunset and sunset after sunrise; A feeling of a lost soul would slowly eat up the only soul that from the skies above he was asked to keep saint and alive so a supernatural presence could dwell in it and take him where no other could have ever had...

Fight to earn your point, yet remember not to hurt...an echo he heard. On bended knees, with a silence as the one of a lamb resting next to a peaceful stream his being would not reflect nor compare but attempt to be.

...Beat after beat...his heartbeats would not shatter the silence but deepen the silence.

The same way a heart calleth love...the same way the depth calleth the deep; his silence would deepen itself...Questions, answers, suppositions every opposing heart, soul and mind ...

His silence one would say...speechless it was leaving them.

His silence another would say...I got no words, why his silence is among us.
H
is silence! None understood, yet, in silence, he stood for speechless was not the word, and again he saw the sunset yet still his heart, soul and mind were...

That that is, if it is only if, his intelligence understood as he walked out of the condo taking the engagement ring Angela had painfully removed from her finger but judged best to do.

Finale

Well, it's been said and done. I am pretty sure that your critic is boiling in your brain and you want to voice it out! I truly appreciate that, but prior to you doing so, let me give you my final thought.

Some of you are still single, some divorced, separated and some married for decades and others it's been a few months...but whatever the case, it is important for you to understand the logic behind the pages you just read; It is not forbidden to be sexually active, however it is forbidden to be if you do not have the pre-requisite!

Will society look at you weird? Trust me; if you end up with a sexually transmitted disease_I think I don't need to go there because we all know the outcome and the impact it will have on ones reputation and health.

On the other hand, having a kid outside wedlock, today, the traditional people will definitely look at you weird and that is whether you are a man or a woman! The more liberal people will simply tease you and label you "Baby Mama" or "Daddy can't get his life together".

Being a single parent is no easy task; I truly and respectfully give a bow to those who are because it's a lot and a huge responsibility.

Do I encourage divorce? No I do not; however do I encourage someone who is being abused to stay in a marriage or relationship…I do not, I will probably be the one to fight so you get out of it! (There are various ways to get out…)

Will I accept one to commit adultery? Certainly NOT; however if the concerned person finds it right to forgive the offender…so be it between them and God, not between them and us who look from outside not knowing fully what happens in that household.

Remember this…when a man and a woman unite in marriage, or begin to date, or when they are engaged _ it is between the two of them! Not between them and the "us" around them. Of course, we are happy (for the most part) when two people we know decide to form a union_ so let us maintain that happiness in rough and easy times!

Men, stay faithful to your women. Women stay faithful to your men.

Men, don't be scared to share with your women your fears_ ego is part of us but conquering that ego makes us real men indeed!

Women, don't be scared to be submissive to your men_ it's not like you are worth nothing when you do, it simply shows that you acknowledge and respect him for who he is.

Men, when women are submissive, it does not mean: Take advantage! It does not mean abuse of her_ remember, she is your lady, your you! So, do it right ma man!

Women, when men share their fears with you, when men drop their ego because they know the value that has been given to you by God as stated in Proverbs 31_ It does not mean that you can mouth talk him in front of your girls, your parents, your kids…come on now…he is your Man, your only one you!

If you are a parent and have not taken the time to seat your unmarried son(s) and or daughter(s) and have a real talk…well the clock is ticking…you better do it soon, as in real soon.

If your parents have not taken the time to talk to you about this sought after topic, well offer them this book…they will get the hint lol

Daughters and Sons, respect your parents! Being a Hypocrite will kill you softly but surely. If you think hiding your run around with men or women outside of your parents house will not catch up to you…Guess what? HAHAHA, you are fooling yourself. A parent will know your doings; they will address it once, twice, and then let you be, let you continue in your debauchery lifestyle.

However, when your sour treat will come your way…I hope that day you are as strong as you think you are while you are hiding and perfecting your hypocrite behavior.

Don't use God as a cover up for your foolish behaviors! Too many of you use the phrase – God knows, I am just being me.

I suggest you stopped. God is not to be used as a token of mockery or a token to shut people up when they give you advise and tell you the truth that you are running away from.

Be wise; change your ways, because everyone's days are numbered!

This being said, I am ready to read your critics and points of view!

Feel free to drop a line on the amazon page of this novel.

Until the next episode, it's not over until my last breath!

Blaise K. Tshibwabwa

TITLES of Malachi Publications

-Spiritual Warfare by Apostle Debbie-Banda

-Kajomona by Blaise Tshibwabwa

-Don't Give Up by Blaise Tshibwabwa

-JL by Blaise Tshibwabwa

-Ignite by Blaise Tshibwabwa

-Moses, Elijah and You
by Blaise Tshibwabwa

-Lethal Weapon by Blaise Tshibwabwa

- Esther by Blaise Tshibwabwa

- Epicurean Living by Lohi Ogolo

www.ingramcontent.com/pod-product-compliance
Lightning Source LLC
Chambersburg PA
CBHW061944070426
42450CB00007BA/1046